My Family Tree

Research Plan

By Catherine Coulter

My Family Tree Research Plan

Copyright© 2014 Catherine Coulter

ISBN-13: 978-1501001789

ISBN-10: 1501001787

Other workbooks in The Family Tree Research Workbook series

Written By Catherine Coulter

Land Research Records

Census Research Record

My Family Research Plan

Military Research Records

Web Log and Web Accounts

Immigration Research Records

Court House Research Records

Family Group Research Record

Naturalization Research Records

My Family Tree Research Record

My Family Tree Research Notebook

Cemetery and Funeral Home Research Records

Let this workbook series help you while Following the Path of Your Ancestors.

The Documents and Records

The path to finding your ancestors starts at home with you. You gather the information on yourself and then you move on to your parents and grandparents and continue down the path. You will find out what information you are missing and need to find. This is the information you will need to start looking for. As you fill in the missing pieces and work backwards you are gathering information that will be used to search for the next generation or two.

Maybe you already have in mind an ancestor that you want to research and don't really want to work on the generation before them. You need to keep in mind though that the information you gather along your way to this ancestor will be the information that you will use to find them and the answers you are looking for. Also, by starting with yourself and working backwards will create a path that will lead you to more information and the ability to confirm facts to insure you have found the right person.

You will find that there are many forks along the road to finding an ancestor that can lead you down the wrong path. The information you gather along your way will help to keep you on the correct one. Once such fork in the road, is that there will be two or more people with the same name living close to each other (as in the same county or possibly the same township). This could lead you down the wrong path if you don't have the information needed to distinguish who is who. They could be related or not. It will be up to you to find out by using the information you have gathered along your way to them.

Some of the many facts about a person's life that are of interest to a genealogist are records of : Birth, Death, Obituaries, Cemeteries, Funeral Homes, Burial, Marriage, Divorce, Immigration, Naturalization, Residences, Military enlistments, Land/deeds, Occupations, Religion, Education, Migration. These are just a few of the many facts that can be found for your ancestor that will eventually bring your family history to life.

There are many documents, records and sources of information that can help you gather the right facts that will aid you in your research. Some of these may be found in your own home or perhaps another family member will have them. If not then the search is on to see if you can find them elsewhere. You may find that you will have to contact or visit churches, court houses, libraries, historical societies, and national or state archives to achieve this.

You will find that your research will need a few items to help you along your path. Below you will find a few suggestions of books, forms, and desk items that will come in handy and you will find useful.

Desk	Forms	Books
Calculator	Research Plan	My Family Research Plan
Magnifying glass		My Family Tree Research Workbook
Highlighters	Family Group Sheets	Family Group Research Records
Pens	Census	Census Research Record
White out	Cemetery	Cemetery and Funeral Home Research Records
Sticky notes	Funeral Home	
Calendar	Birth	Court House Research Records
Paper clips	Death	
Paper clamps	Marriage	
Binders	Land	Land Research Records
File folders	Military	Military Research Records
File jackets	Immigration	Immigration Research Records
Dividers	Naturalization	Naturalization Research Records
Labels	Web log	Web Log and Web Account
Hole punch	Interview	My Family Research Plan
Envelopes	Research Note Book	My Family Tree Research Notebook
Stamps	Family Tree Chart	
Note cards		
Note card file box		
Note card file box tabs		

Organization is important. It will help keep your information together and make it easy to find facts and information you want to look at. A good organization system takes a while to get set up and it can be quite personalized as you wish to make it. When I started out, I was using index cards. Now I have written a series of books listed in the chart on the previous page that I use whether I am doing research for myself or for others. The forms keep me apprised of what I know and what I need to research. They also help me to record the information I find. That is what you need to have, a system that works well for you and makes your research easy and fits well with your research style. Maybe these books and forms would before you. I also use binders and file folders as well as a computer. A computer program is a great tool as well that can generate reports from the information you put into it about your family. Do not hesitate to try a new organization system or combine several different ones. When you have a system that works well you will be able to accomplish more research in less time without researching for the same information more than once. At least part of the organizational system you use should be able to be transported to where ever your research takes you. It should be easy to carry and insure you will not lose pages and information from it as you move about. Losing information or having it become disorganized can lead to more time wasted in finding or reorganizing it.

Having your research organized will also help you with documenting the places (sources) you have found the information. This is very important for several reasons. The first reason to document your sources of information is that if you were to share the information with someone else they would like to know where you found it so they too may view the original source of the information themselves. Secondly, you may find that you need to go back to reconfirm some information yourself. Thirdly, having this documentation insures that it is accurate. Fourthly, you will be able to use it as proof that your information that is correct should you need to.

For a web site I always add the website itself to the start of my notes. I like to add the name of the web site the data base used if there was one. I have found I have gone back to the website for more information or to be able to share it with someone else. You will find that when sharing your family information with someone that they are more likely to accept information being correct if you can prove it with the source of the information.

I also caution you to do the same. When looking at information on an ancestor that someone else has done you need to view the source or research it yourself to confirm that the fact that it is accurate. Unintentional mistakes can be made and information always should be verified before accepting it as a part of your family tree. This is even if you find it on a website such as Ancestry.com or some other site.

Here is a list of 16 mistakes to avoid that will cause you problems

There are some mistakes that can be made when starting to research your family history that you should be aware of. Below are twelve of the more common ones that are typically made by those new to genealogy.

1. The first one is **not getting and using family group sheets**. These group sheets are an important research tool that will help you to keep track of the information you already have and what you need to look for. They will be the foundation of your research plan.
2. **Not being organized** is a necessity in genealogy that can be over looked at first. Well organized records will keep you from repeating research you have already completed or losing documents and information.
3. The next mistake that can be made is **not keeping a copy** of your information at home during your research trips. Information can be lost or miss placed. You need to make sure you have a backup copy in case something happens to your working copy.
4. **Not making photo copies** of documents and records you find is important and often neglected. Thinking that because you write it down some where the information you find on them is good enough can be a mistake. One that will send you in search of it again.
5. **Not keeping track of where you find your information** and creating a cite list is also a big mistake that is often made. A cite listing for every document and information you find will save you time and trouble if you need to go back to the source for more information or to confirm for others where you got the information from.
6. Some beginning researchers will **not think of the histories** in the area their ancestors lived in. In the histories you may be able to find an ancestors biography, information on your ancestor as it relates the history in that area.

7. **Not finding out the time table for the formation of the County and townships** in the area your ancestor lived. These will determine where to look for documents and information on your ancestor.

8. Be aware of the fact that **some of these "histories" may contain mistakes** or information that someone other than the actual ancestor *told* to the author of the book. Mistakes can be made. You need to verify information that you find or are given to insure its accuracy. If not you could be led down the wrong path and run into a brick wall causing you to retrace your steps. This includes other family histories a relative or someone else has done as well. Always be excited over the information but be cautious and verify the information any way.

9. This mistake can be very easily over looked. The **spelling of your ancestor's names could be different than what you have and n**ot realizing this could cause you problems. There can also be errors and mistakes made on documents and done by transcribers like you need to be watchful for. Also you need to be mindful of the fact that ancestor's names may have been changed at some point with the spelling or changed in other ways.

10. **Not considering using an ancestor's middle name or nick name** as a first in researching.

11. **Believing every detail in a family story** that has been handed down through the generations in your family. As in the children's game Telephone the story is likely to have changed by the time it reaches you. That's not saying that it is all wrong. You just need to make sure you verify the details before accepting them as fact.

12. **Do not trust that all information is accurate**. For example ages on census records could very well be off by a year or two or even more if the person giving the information was not sure of the age.

13. Do not assume if it's on the internet that it's true. Verify Verify Verify

14. The biggest mistake you can do when doing genealogy is not to talk to family members about the family. The information, documents, and stories are often lost when this step is not done. Once you have talk to someone in your family do not assume you have all they remember in one conversation. My Grandmother was full of stories and information she was willing to share but from the time I was a child she would share them with us. She continued to tell different stories as we grew up. It was rare for her to share one more than once unless asked to.

15. When dealing with theories, remember that they are just that Theories at least until you can prove otherwise. Theories are great tools but they are not facts.
16. **Giving up.** Do not give up. The last one that I am going to mention here is quitting when you hit a brick wall and you will hit a brick wall sometime. We all do. You can find a path around that wall if you are persistent enough. Even if it means you leave that ancestor or surname for a time to work on another one and then come back to it.

When dealing with maps its best to find the history of the map itself as well. There is a Map of Wolf Creek Mercer Count Pa what was created in the late 1800's that is called a land owner map. The map dose not list Carson Coulter as owning the land He was living on at that time. It gives his Brother's name instead. The map is itself wrong. I know this because the land records for Carson Coulter to verify that the land belonged to him instead at the time the map was created and not his brother. So it is very exciting to find your ancestors name on a land owner's map but be aware you still need to check land records to verify that the map is correct. Don't just assume that it is.

It is advisable to consider the history of the area, township, and county where your ancestors lived and the time period in which they were there. You never know what kind of information you will find that will make your family history come alive or where it could lead you. For example, the date that the township or county was formed and from where it was created from could help you to information on your ancestors. A township formed from another one could mean that though as of today they would have lived in one town ship at the time they actually lived there they were in a different township altogether. Most importantly though is the county boundaries If a new county was formed from an older one all the records that were created while their home was considered to be in the older county .would stay with the older county and any new ones made would then be with the new county.

Do not forget to research land records as well. They have the potential to reveal information you may not find elsewhere. One such piece of information can be who they bought or sold the land from / to. Another relative could have very well have been involved. If so then you will have found another stepping stone on the path of your ancestors.

How to Use this Planner

On the first page add the surname of the family you intend to research. Then fill in the information of the names of the family members you are going to research and give them a number for example:

Ancestor's Name __William Thomas_____# __1___

If your ancestor is female and she married into this surname you can add her full name including her *maiden name* as seen below

Ancestor's Name ___Jane *Mc Crumb* Wick_____# ___2__

The numbering of ancestors names will give you a reference number to use in the Family Members Contacted section of this planner as well as being able to attach it to any other information you may add in this book or the other books in this series. It will give you a guide to help you navigate your collection of notes and information as you find them. Also if you happen to have two ancestors with the same name (if one was named after another) you can use this number to keep the information connected to the right ancestor.

Most of the sections are self-explanatory. They are checklists of information you can use to plan what you would like to research next or just to keep track of what you have already done. There are lists for you to complete such as questions you wish to ask a family member during an interview. Keeping this record will help you to avoid repeating research you have already competed and keep you on your path to finding the answers you are in need of. It will help you to figure out what you need to do.

Research Plan for the Surname of: _____

Names researching with in this family

Ancestor's First Name_____ #_____

Ancestor's First Name_____ #_____

Ancestor's First Name_____ #_____

Ancestor's First Name_____ #_____

Ancestor's First Name_____ #_____

Ancestor's First Name_____ #_____

Ancestor's First Name_____ #_____

Ancestor's First Name_____ #_____

Ancestor's First Name_____ #_____

Ancestor's First Name_____ #_____

Notes:

Information and Records Your Family May Have

Announcements
Wedding
Birth
Anniversary
Graduation

Certificates/ Documents/ Records
Birth
Wedding
Anniversary
Graduation
Any type of Achievement
Death
Divorce
Adoption
Will
Report Cards
Memorial Cards
Baptism
Social Security Card
Apprenticeship Records
Deeds
Land Grants
Awards
Guardian Papers
Naturalization Papers

Books
Baby Books	Wedding Books
Funeral	School Year
Family Bibles	Scrap Books
Diary / Journal	Photo Album

News Papers
Birth
Wedding
Anniversary
Graduation
Achievement
Death
Divorce
Stories / Articles
Sports
Obituaries
Honor Rolls
Awards

Personal Papers
Letters
Photographs
Post Cards

Military Records
Service Records
Pension Records
Service Medals
Ribbons
Insignias
Discharge Records

Other
Genealogies
Histories

Documents For_____ #_____

- ☐ Family Letters
- ☐ Family Bible
- ☐ Marriage Certificates
- ☐ Birth Certificates
- ☐ Death Certificates
- ☐ Baptism Certificates
- ☐ Photo Albums
- ☐ _____
- ☐ _____
- ☐ _____
- ☐ _____
- ☐ _____
- ☐ _____
- ☐ _____
- ☐ _____
- ☐ _____
- ☐ _____
- ☐ _____
- ☐ _____

Notes:

Documents For_____#_____

- ☐ Family Letters
- ☐ Family Bible
- ☐ Marriage Certificates
- ☐ Birth Certificates
- ☐ Death Certificates
- ☐ Baptism Certificates
- ☐ Photo Albums
- ☐ _____
- ☐ _____
- ☐ _____
- ☐ _____
- ☐ _____
- ☐ _____
- ☐ _____
- ☐ _____
- ☐ _____
- ☐ _____
- ☐ _____
- ☐ _____

Notes:

Documents For_____ #_____

- ☐ Family Letters
- ☐ Family Bible
- ☐ Marriage Certificates
- ☐ Birth Certificates
- ☐ Death Certificates
- ☐ Baptism Certificates
- ☐ Photo Albums
- ☐ _____
- ☐ _____
- ☐ _____
- ☐ _____
- ☐ _____
- ☐ _____
- ☐ _____
- ☐ _____
- ☐ _____
- ☐ _____
- ☐ _____
- ☐ _____

Notes:

Documents For_____#_____

- ☐ Family Letters
- ☐ Family Bible
- ☐ Marriage Certificates
- ☐ Birth Certificates
- ☐ Death Certificates
- ☐ Baptism Certificates
- ☐ Photo Albums
- ☐ _____
- ☐ _____
- ☐ _____
- ☐ _____
- ☐ _____
- ☐ _____
- ☐ _____
- ☐ _____
- ☐ _____
- ☐ _____
- ☐ _____
- ☐ _____

Notes:

Documents For_____#_____

- ☐ Family Letters
- ☐ Family Bible
- ☐ Marriage Certificates
- ☐ Birth Certificates
- ☐ Death Certificates
- ☐ Baptism Certificates
- ☐ Photo Albums
- ☐ _____
- ☐ _____
- ☐ _____
- ☐ _____
- ☐ _____
- ☐ _____
- ☐ _____
- ☐ _____
- ☐ _____
- ☐ _____
- ☐ _____

Notes:

Documents For_____ **#**_____

- ☐ Family Letters
- ☐ Family Bible
- ☐ Marriage Certificates
- ☐ Birth Certificates
- ☐ Death Certificates
- ☐ Baptism Certificates
- ☐ Photo Albums
- ☐ _____
- ☐ _____
- ☐ _____
- ☐ _____
- ☐ _____
- ☐ _____
- ☐ _____
- ☐ _____
- ☐ _____
- ☐ _____
- ☐ _____
- ☐ _____

Notes:

Family members to contact:

☐ _____Ancestor #_____Date contacted_____
about_____
_____
_____
_____

☐ _____Ancestor #_____Date contacted_____
about_____
_____
_____
_____

☐ _____Ancestor #_____Date contacted_____
about_____
_____
_____
_____

☐ _____Ancestor #_____Date contacted_____
about_____
_____
_____
_____

☐ _____Ancestor #_____Date contacted_____
about_____
_____
_____
_____

☐ _____Ancestor #_____Date contacted_____
about_____
_____
_____
_____

☐ _____Ancestor #_____Date contacted_____
about_____
_____
_____
_____

Churches

- ☐ _____ #____
- ☐ _____ #____
- ☐ _____ #____
- ☐ _____ #____
- ☐ _____ #____
- ☐ _____ #____

Cemeteries

- ☐ _____ #____
- ☐ _____ #____
- ☐ _____ #____
- ☐ _____ #____
- ☐ _____ #____
- ☐ _____ #____

Court Houses

- ☐ _____ #____
- ☐ _____ #____
- ☐ _____ #____
- ☐ _____ #____
- ☐ _____ #____

Funeral Homes

- ☐ _____ #____
- ☐ _____ #____
- ☐ _____ #____
- ☐ _____ #____
- ☐ _____ #____

Resources from _____ **Historical Society**

- ☐ Cemeteries
- ☐ Family Histories
- ☐ Newspaper Clippings
- ☐ House Photos
- ☐ City Directories
- ☐ Year Books from high school and college
- ☐ Family Files and Binders
- ☐ Cenus Records
- ☐ _____
- ☐ _____
- ☐ _____
- ☐ _____
- ☐ _____
- ☐ _____
- ☐ _____

Books

- [ ] _____
- [ ] _____
- [ ] _____
- [ ] _____
- [ ] _____
- [ ] _____
- [ ] _____
- [ ] _____
- [ ] _____
- [ ] _____
- [ ] _____
- [ ] _____
- [ ] _____
- [ ] _____
- [ ] _____
- [ ] _____
- [ ] _____
- [ ] _____
- [ ] _____
- [ ] _____
- [ ] _____
- [ ] _____
- [ ] _____
- [ ] _____
- [ ] _____
- [ ] _____
- [ ] _____
- [ ] _____
- [ ] _____
- [ ] _____
- [ ] _____

The internet has become a large part of genealogy research today. There are many Internet sites these days for you to use in your genealogy research. Some of the sites are free and others have a fee attached to them. They are all useful and full of information. The search engine on a computer is also a great tool to use as well. You will find below some of the web sites that may be of some use to you if you care to try them. I have also included a form for you to fill out as you are using the various internet web sites. For example:

Site____www.ancestory.com_____

Data Base Used

- 1860 Census Mercer County Pa____
- 1870 Census Mercer County Pa____
- _____
- _____

Internet Sites
- Ancestry
- Roots Web Sites
- Interment.net
- Us Gen Web
- Cyndi's List
- Google Books
- Mercer County Genealogy Trails
- Find a Grave
- Family Search
- Castle Garden
- Ellis Island
- Genealogy Trails
- Google Books
- National Archives

- _____
- _____
- _____
- _____
- _____
- _____
- _____
- _____
- _____
- _____
- _____
- _____
- _____
- _____
- _____
- _____
- _____
- _____

Site_____

Data Base Used

      ○ _____

      ○ _____

      ○ _____

      ○ _____

      ○ _____

Site_____

Data Base Used

      ○ _____

      ○ _____

      ○ _____

      ○ _____

      ○ _____

Site_____

Data Base Used

      ○ _____

      ○ _____

      ○ _____

      ○ _____

      ○ _____

Site_____

Data Base Used

      ○ _____

      ○ _____

      ○ _____

      ○ _____

      ○ _____

Site_____

Data Base Used

- ○ _____
- ○ _____
- ○ _____
- ○ _____
- ○ _____

Site_____

Data Base Used

- ○ _____
- ○ _____
- ○ _____
- ○ _____
- ○ _____

Site_____

Data Base Used

- ○ _____
- ○ _____
- ○ _____
- ○ _____
- ○ _____

Site_____

Data Base Used

- ○ _____
- ○ _____
- ○ _____
- ○ _____
- ○ _____

Announcements
- ☐ Wedding
- ☐ Birth
- ☐ Anniversary
- ☐ Graduation

Certificates/ Documents/ Records
- ☐ Birth
- ☐ Wedding
- ☐ Anniversary
- ☐ Graduation
- ☐ Achievement
- ☐ Death
- ☐ Divorce
- ☐ Adoption
- ☐ Will
- ☐ Report Cards
- ☐ Memorial Cards
- ☐ Baptism
- ☐ Social Security Card
- ☐ Apprenticeship Records
- ☐ Deeds
- ☐ Land Grants
- ☐ Awards
- ☐ Guardian Papers
- ☐ Naturalization Papers

Books
- ☐ Baby
- ☐ Wedding
- ☐ Funeral
- ☐ School Year Books
- ☐ Family Bibles

- ☐ Scrap Books
- ☐ Diary / Journal
- ☐ Photograph Albums

News paper
- ☐ Birth
- ☐ Wedding
- ☐ Anniversary
- ☐ Graduation
- ☐ Achievement
- ☐ Death
- ☐ Divorce
- ☐ Stories / Articles
- ☐ Sports
- ☐ Obituaries
- ☐ Honor rolls
- ☐ Awards

Personal papers
- ☐ Letters
- ☐ Photographs
- ☐ Post Cards
- ☐ Memberships

Military Records
- ☐ Service Records
- ☐ Pension Records
- ☐ Service Medals
- ☐ Ribbons
- ☐ Insignias
- ☐ Discharge Records

Talking to family about them and your ancestors

You will need to ask specific questions about people, events, or dates. This will help the person you are asking to be able to give you the answers you are hoping to find. The questions that are the most important to you should be asked first. Create you list of questions with that in mind and check off the ones you have finished so if you have to go back and ask more you will not be repeating ones you don't want to. You will also want to make notes about other questions that may arise during the interview.

You never know what may occur to keep you from finishing the interview. Some relatives may not be up to spending the afternoon going over their lives but are willing to do so for a shorter period of time. You may have to spread your questions out over several days in order to go over all of them. You never know you may ask one question and get the next one your list answered as well without it being asked.

If you are talking to an older person keep in mind what they remember today they very well may not remember at a later date. It also goes the other way around as well, what they do not remember today they may remember tomorrow or another day. You might want to consider doing an interview over a course of several days.

If they do not remember some of the questions that are most important to you do not constantly ask them every day give them some time perhaps a week later or longer would do. The last thing you want to do is frustrate them by asking the same question over and over again. Find a different question that will give you the information you are looking for. Sometimes that is all it takes is a different way to ask. If you have photographs or an object such as an heirloom that you can show them and talk about you may find not only the information you are looking for but a very interesting story to go along with the photo or heirloom.

There are several ways to record the information you receive from the interview. You should take notes by writing the answer to your question and anything else you find helpful. But, you can also video record the interview or use a voice recorder as well. If you chose to record your interview you need to ask permission to do so. If you do record it, be sure to place the recorder in a place that is unobtrusive but will be able to record the conversation clearly. This will help the interviewee to relax and not focus on being recorded.

In order to identify who you were talking to when recording an interview you should have them say their name and the date the recording is being done. If you feel uncomfortable asking this questions you could put on the recording yourself before the meeting the name, date, and age of the person you are meeting. This will help you keep track of who you talked to when you did so and it will not mix up two different people. You will also be able to find the recording much easier as well. At the end of the interview be sure to say a phrase such as thank you, (their Name), for talking to me or we are ending the recording now. Something to let you and them know the interview is over and that the recording is being stopped. It will help you to know where you ended with that person.

You will need to have a list of questions you will hope to get answered. When you start the interview session there are a few questions below you may want to start with.

When and where were you born?

What are the names of your parents and their siblings?

Do you know the names of your grandparents and their siblings?

What year were they born in?

Where did you grow up?

What kind of jobs did you have?

Were you ever in the military?

If you were then what branch Army, Air Force, Marines, National Guard, or other_____?

Keep in mind that the questions you should ask should be specific. For example instead of asking what do you know about your grandfather? You ask instead, what was your grandfather job. These specific questions are will help lead the interview in the direction you want it to go and hopefully give you the answers you are looking for. Your questions should give you information that you need so you can write a description or to aid you in your research. Its best to review what information you are lacking and see if you can find it or something that will lead you to more. You also may want to hear what it was like to live through an event such as the depression or some other event that would make history of that time period come alive for you and your family. It also could reveal facts that you may not have thought of as well.

Some of the questions you may want to consider asking are:

Where you named after someone and if so who? Why?
If you were did you know that person and what were they like?
Do you have a favorite childhood memory?
What kind of chores did you have growing up?
Were there any family stories about the family?
What was the name of your school and where was it located?
Do you have a favorite holiday and why is it your favorite?
Do you have a holiday that you do not like and why?
Do you know your grandparents names and where they came from?
How did you meet your husband /wife?
How did you ask or were asked to marry?
When and where did you get married?
After you were married where did you first live?
Who in your family worked to support the family?
Where did they work?
What kind of health issues run in the family?
Do you know if the spelling of the surname name changed over time?
Who's the oldest relative you remember (and what do you remember about him or her)?
How did your parents meet?
How did you meet your spouse?
A good question to help end an interview is to ask: Before I go is there anything else you would like to add to the family history?

On the Next three pages you will be able to fill in the name of the person you wish to interview the date of the interview and a recording number it you are going to record it. There is room for 11 questions per person to help you get started.

Name_____ Date_____ Recording #_____

1. _____
   _____
   _____
   _____

2. _____
   _____
   _____
   _____

3. _____
   _____
   _____
   _____

4. _____
   _____
   _____
   _____

5. _____
   _____
   _____
   _____

6. _____
   _____
   _____
   _____

7. _____
   _____
   _____
   _____

Name_____ Date_____ Recording #_____

1. _____
_____
_____
_____

2. _____
_____
_____
_____

3. _____
_____
_____
_____

4. _____
_____
_____
_____

5. _____
_____
_____
_____

6. _____
_____
_____
_____

7. _____
_____
_____
_____

Name_____ Date_____ Recording #_____

1. _____
_____
_____
_____

2. _____
_____
_____
_____

3. _____
_____
_____
_____

4. _____
_____
_____
_____

5. _____
_____
_____
_____

6. _____
_____
_____
_____

7. _____
_____
_____
_____

Name_____ Date_____ Recording #_____

1. _____
   _____
   _____
   _____

2. _____
   _____
   _____
   _____

3. _____
   _____
   _____
   _____

4. _____
   _____
   _____
   _____

5. _____
   _____
   _____
   _____

6. _____
   _____
   _____
   _____

7. _____
   _____
   _____
   _____

Name_____ Date_____ Recording #_____

1. _____
   _____
   _____
   _____

2. _____
   _____
   _____
   _____

3. _____
   _____
   _____
   _____

4. _____
   _____
   _____
   _____

5. _____
   _____
   _____
   _____

6. _____
   _____
   _____
   _____

7. _____
   _____
   _____
   _____

January

Sun	Mon	Tue	Wed	Thu	Fri	Sat

NOTES

NOTES:_____

February

Sun	Mon	Tue	Wed	Thu	Fri	Sat

NOTES

NOTES:_____

March

Sun	Mon	Tue	Wed	Thu	Fri	Sat

NOTES

NOTES:

April

Sun	Mon	Tue	Wed	Thu	Fri	Sat

NOTES

NOTES:

May

Sun	Mon	Tue	Wed	Thu	Fri	Sat

NOTES

NOTES:

June

Sun	Mon	Tue	Wed	Thu	Fri	Sat

NOTES

NOTES:

July

Sun	Mon	Tue	Wed	Thu	Fri	Sat

NOTES

NOTES:

August

Sun	Mon	Tue	Wed	Thu	Fri	Sat

NOTES

NOTES:

September

Sun	Mon	Tue	Wed	Thu	Fri	Sat

NOTES

NOTES:

October

Sun	Mon	Tue	Wed	Thu	Fri	Sat

NOTES

NOTES:

November

Sun	Mon	Tue	Wed	Thu	Fri	Sat

NOTES

NOTES:

December

Sun	Mon	Tue	Wed	Thu	Fri	Sat

NOTES

NOTES:

NOTES:

NOTES:

NOTES: